SAFINAT AL-NAJA

SAFINAT AL-NAJA

A CONCISE MANUAL OF ISLAMIC SACRED LAW

Second edition

Safinat al-Najā
A concise manual of Islamic sacred law
Sālim b. 'Abdullah b. Sa'd b. Sumair al-Haḍramī

ISBN: 978 0 9565874 0 4

The Ribat Institute
PO Box 1352, Woking, Surrey. GU22 2GH
www.ribat.org.uk
info@ribat.org.uk

Cover design Tareq Miah

Typography quemedia.co.uk, info@quemedia.co.uk

Printed in the UK by Biddles.

The book is printed using FSC certified paper

Mixed Sources
Product group from well-managed forests, controlled sources and recycled wood or fiber
FSC
www.fsc.org Cert no. TT-COC-002303
© 1996 Forest Stewardship Council

Translator's note - All Islamic measurement conversions have been taken from the manual, Reliance of the Traveller (revised edition 1997), Ibn Naqīb al-Misrī (trans. Nuh Ha Mīm Keller). Minor parts of the original Arabic text of *Safinat al-Najā* have been left untranslated for the purposes of relevancy. These parts have been placed between parentheses in the original Arabic.

Contents

The Author 13

Foreword 15

Al-Ḥabīb 'Ali Mash-hūr b. Ḥafīẓ 15

Shaykh 'Umar b. Husayn al-Khaṭīb 17

Pillars of Islam 22

Pillars of faith 22

The Book of Purification 24

Puberty 24

Bathroom etiquette 25

Ablution 26

Intention 26

Water measurements 27

Purificatory bath 28

Conditions of ablution 29

Nullification of ablution 30

Earth ablution 33

Nullification of the earth ablution 36

Impurities transformed 36

Impurities 37

Menstruation 39

The Book of Prayer 40

Excuses 40

Prayer conditions 41

Ritual impurities 41
Nakedness 42
Pillars of prayer 42
Intention 44
Conditions of Allahu Akbar 45
Conditions of the Fātiḥa 46
Raising hands in prayer 48
Conditions for prostration 48
Emphases 50
Prayer times 50
Impermissible prayer times 52
Pauses 53
Stillness 54
Prostrating out of absentmindedness 55
Principal sunnas 56
Invalidation of prayer 56
Intention for leading prayer 58
Conditions for following 58
Joining prayers 61
Shortening prayers 62
Friday prayer 63

THE BOOK OF FUNERAL LAW 66
Washing 66
Shrouding 67

Prayer 67
Burial 68
Seeking assistance 69

THE BOOK OF ZAKĀT 71
Zakāt categories 71
Livestock 72
Gold & silver 73
Crops 73
Trade merchandise 74
Buried gold & silver 75
Mined gold & silver 75
Zakāt al-Fiṭr 76

THE BOOK OF FASTING 78
Obligation to fast 78
Conditions of validity 79
Conditions of obligation 80
Pillars of fasting 81
Major expiation 81
Making up missed fasts 82
Invalidation of the fast 83
Rulings of breaking the fast 84
Things ingested which do not break the fast 86

مَن يُرِد اللهُ به خيراً يُفَقِّهْهُ في الدِّين

حديث شريف

THE AUTHOR

He is the distinguished, the erudite, the judge and jurist, Shaikh Sālim b. 'Abdullah b. Sa'd b. Sumair al-Haḍramī al-Shāfi'ī. Born in the village Dhī Asba, from amongst the villages of the valley of Hadramaut.

He was raised and educated under the tutelage of his father, Shaikh 'Abdullah b. Sa'd b. Sumair, under whom he completed the noble Qur'ān and perfected its disciplines. Thereafter he excelled in the art of recitation (*al-iqrā'*), and hence was given the title '*al-Mu'allim*' [The Instructor], this being a haḍramī term applied to one instructing in the art of recitation of the Noble Qur'ān, drawing from the prophetic tradition of 'Uthmān b. 'Affān ﷺ, 'The best of you are those who learn the Qur'ān and teach it.'

He studied law under his father, and other scholars, from Hadramaut in the thirteenth century. From amongst them was 'Umar b. Saqqāf b. Muḥammad b. 'Umar b. Ṭāha al-Ṣafi, 'Umar b. Zain b. Sumaiṭ and others.

He propagated and taught the various disciplines, and students approached him from far and wide taking their first sips from his spring of knowledge. From the most prominent of his students was the sayyid al-Ḥabīb 'Abdullah b. Ṭāha al-Ḥaddār al-Ḥaddād and Shaikh 'Alī b. 'Umar Bā-Gawza. Thereafter his reputation spread, to the extent that poetry was comprised in praise of him by peers such as Shaikh 'Abdullah Aḥmad Bā-Sudan.

Alongside his broad legal erudition he engaged in politics and was also an expert in munitions. He was commissioned to the Kathariya state, in India to vet army experts in the field of defence. He was also charged with the purchase of modern military weaponry from Singapore, which he had shipped to Hadramaut. Furthermore the protocol between the people of Yāfi' and the Kathiriya State was also administered under his guidance.

Therefter Shaikh Sālim was elected as an advisor to Sultan 'Abdullah b. Muḥsin, with there being no decree executed except under his consultation. However upon an altercation Sultan 'Abdullah ceased referring to him for consultation and Shaikh Sālim consequently travelled to India, and then onto Java, Indonesia where he took up residency.

He was known to be from amongst the pious, reciting the book of God often. Shaikh Aḥmad Hadrāwī al-Makkī mentioned that he would complete a recitation of the Qur'ān whilst circumambulating the House of God (in Mecca). It was in Bitawa, from amongst the locales of Java, that death grasped him in the year 1271/1854. He died bequeathing many works, from them *Safīnat al-Najā* and also *Fawā'id al-Jaliyya fī al-Zajr 'an Ta'āṭī al-Ḥiyal al-Ribawīyya.* May God have mercy upon him, amīn. [1]

[1] This biography was taken from the original Arabic text which itself quotes from *al-Dura al-Taymiya* by al-Sayyid 'Umar b. Ḥāmid al-Jilānī.

FOREWORD

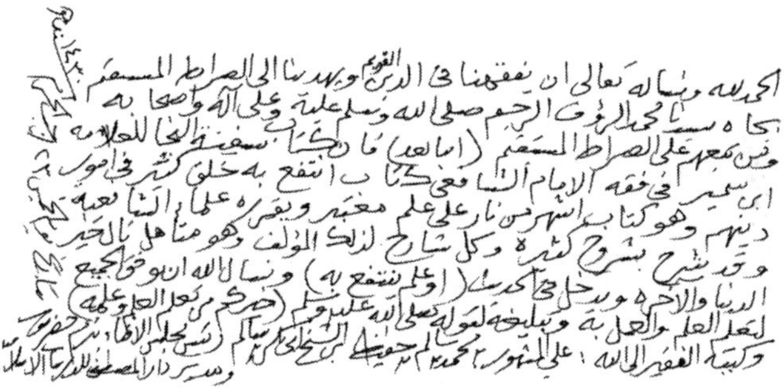
الحمد لله ونسأله تعالى أن يفقهنا في الدين القويم ويهدينا إلى الصراط المستقيم
بجاه سيدنا محمد الرؤوف الرحيم صلى الله وسلم عليه وعلى آله وأصحابه
ومن تبعهم على الصراط المستقيم (أما بعد) فإن كتاب سفينة النجا للعلامة
ابن سمير في فقه الإمام الشافعي كتاب انتفع به خلق كثير في أمور
دينهم وهو كتاب أشهر من نار على علم معتبر ويقرره علماء الشافعية
وقد شرح بشروح كثيرة وكل شارح لذلك المؤلف وهو متأهل نال الخير
في الدنيا والآخرة ويدخل في الحديث (أو علم ينتفع به) ونسأل الله أن يوفق الجميع
لتعلم العلم والعمل به وتبليغه لقوله صلى الله عليه وسلم (خيركم من تعلم العلم وعلمه)
وكتبه الفقير إلى الله علي المشهور بن محمد بن حفيظ بن الشيخ أبي بكر بن سالم رئيس مجلس الإفتاء بتريم حضرموت ومدير دار المصطفى للدراسات الإسلامية

All praise is for God. We ask Him, the Most High, to grant us understanding of this true religion and to guide us to the straight path, by the rank of our master, Muḥammad ﷺ the kind and compassionate one. May God send peace and blessings upon him, his Family and Companions, and upon those who have followed them upon the straight path.

The treatise *Safīnat al-Najā*, by the distinguished Ibn Sumair from the juristic school of Imam al-Shāfi'ī, is a book that has been of great benefit to many people with regards to their religious affairs.

Indeed it is a work that has burned more brightly than a beacon on a mountain top. Numerous commentaries have been on written on it, and every qualified commentator has acquired the good of this world and the hereafter, and he falls under the tradition of '*beneficial knowledge*'.[1]

We ask God to bestow divine success in enabling all to undertake the study of knowledge, to act upon this knowledge, and convey it by virtue of his statement ﷺ, '*The finest of you are those who study knowledge and teach it.*' This has been written by the one indebted to God.

'Alī al-Mash-hūr b. Muḥammad b. Sālim b. Ḥafīẓ b. Shaykh Abi Bakr b. Sālim

Head of the Fatwa Council, Tarim, Hadramaut
Director of Studies, Dār al-Muṣṭafa, Institute of Islamic Studies

Thursday 23rd of the inviolable month of Rajab, 1430 a.h.

[1] Muslim, *Wasiya*, 4310. On the authority of Abu Huraira ﷺ that the Prophet ﷺ said, 'When a person passes away, his deeds are severed except for three things, ongoing charity, beneficial knowledge and a pious child who supplicates for him.'

بسم الله الرحمن الرحيم

الحمد لله الذي قدر فهدى والصلاة والسلام على من جمع الله فيه
جميع معاني الهدى سيدنا محمد وآله وأصحابه أنجم الاهتداء.
وبعد: فإن الله عز وجل لا يزال بفضله يظهر في دينه أهل الاهتمام
بنشره وتعاليمه والقيام بواجب حقه ويقذف في قلوب عدد
من هذه الأمة أنوار محبة النفع للآخرين تطلباً لمرضاته ومحبة لمتابعة
نبيه صلى الله عليه وسلم، وهذا ما دعا وحدى أخانا الفاضل المهتم
بنشر الفضائل الشاب المقبل على الخير والمحب لنشره بين الناس:
فائز بن أمير قريشي إلى ترجمة رسالة السفينة في فقه الإمام
الشافعي للعلامة سالم بن سمير الحضرمي وسفينة النجاء من الكتب
التي ظهرت عليها علامات القبول بين المسلمين لا سيما أتباع مذهب
الإمام الشافعي في فروع الفقه فنسأل الله القبول لهذه الترجمة وأن
ينفع بها كما نفع بأصلها وأن يجعل حياة هذا الشاب المترجم عامرة
بالإيمان والنفع للآخرين والعلم والعمل وأن يبارك في أهله
وأولاده وفي جميع المهتمين بهذا الخير وأن يكثر منهم في الأمة إنه ولي
ذلك والقادر عليه

كتبه/ عمر بن حسين بن عمر الخطيب الأنصاري
بتريم/ اليمن/ رمضان ١٤٢٠هـ

In the Name of God, Most Merciful and Compassionate

Praise is for God, who decreed then directed, and blessings and peace upon the one in whom God gathered all meanings of guidance, our liegelord Muḥammad as well as his folk and companions, the stars of guidance.

To proceed. God, Mighty and Majestic, continues through His beneficence to manifest within His religion those with concern for its propagation, for its teachings and for fulfilling its due. He casts into the hearts of a group from this nation the love of benefiting, seeking thereby His pleasure, and [He casts] a love of following His Prophet, may God bless him and grant him peace.

This is what summoned and guided our virtuous brother; who possesses a concern for propagating meritorious deeds; this young man who avidly seeks goodness and loves to spread it among people; Fā'iz b. Amīr Qureshy, to translate the treatise *Safīnat al-Najā* according to the juristic school of Imam al-Shāfiʿī, which was authored by the erudite scholar Sālim b. Sumair al-Haḍramī. *Safīnat al-Najā* is from the books upon which the signs of acceptance among the Muslims are manifest, in particular from amongst the followers of the Shāfiʿī school of jurisprudence.

We ask God to accept this translation and that He bring through it benefit as He did through its original, and [we ask] that He make the life of this young translator thrive with faith, benefit for others, knowledge and practice; and [we ask] that He bless his family, his children and those who show concern for this act of goodness; and [we ask] that He increase the likes of them in this nation. Indeed He is the patron of that and has unlimited power to do so.

ʿUmar b. Ḥusayn b. ʿUmar al-Khaṭīb al-Anṣārī

Tarim, Yemen. Ramaḍān, 1430 a.h
September 2009

IN THE NAME OF GOD THE COMPASSIONATE THE MERCIFUL

Author's Introduction

الحمد لله رب العالمين و به نستعين على أمور الدنيا و الدين و صلى الله و
سلم على سيدنا محمد خاتم النبيين و على آله و صحبه أجمعين و لا حول و
لا قوة إلا بالله العلي العظيم

All praise is for God, Lord of the Worlds. We seek His help in worldly and religious affairs, and may peace and blessings be upon our Master Muḥammad, Seal of the Prophets; and upon his Family and Companions. There is no power, nor strength, save through God, the High the Exalted.

Section 1

فصل : أركان الإسلام خمسة. شهادة أن لا إله إلا الله و أن محمدا رسول الله و
إقام الصلاة و إيتاء الزكاة و صوم رمضان و حج البيت لمن استطاع إليه سبيلا

Section 1: **Pillars of Islam**

There are five pillars of Islam:

1. Testifying that there is no deity save God, and that Muḥammad ﷺ is the Messenger of God;
2. Establishing the Prayer;
3. Paying Zakāt;
4. Fasting the month of Ramaḍān and;
5. Performing the pilgrimage to the House[1], for one who is able.

Section 1a فصل : أركان الإيمان ستة. أن تؤمن بالله و ملائكته و كتبه و رسله وباليوم
الآخر و بالقدر خيره و شره من الله تعالى

Section 1 (a): **Pillars of Faith**

There are six pillars of faith (*īmān*):

To believe in:

1. God;
2. His Angels;
3. His Books;
4. His Messengers;
5. The Last Day, and;
6. Predetermination (*qadr*) the good and bad of it being from God ﷻ.

---

1 i.e. To the Ka'ba in Mecca

فصل : ومعنى لا إله إلا الله لامعبود بحق في الوجود إلا الله .

The meaning of, 'there is no deity save God', is that there is no merit worthy deity in existence except God.

THE BOOK OF PURIFICATION

فصل : علامات البلوغ ثلاثة. تمام خمسة عشرة سنة في الذكر و الأنثى و
SECTION 2 الإحتلام في الذكر و الإنثى لتسع سنين و الحيض في الإنثى لتسع سنين

SECTION 2: **Puberty** *(bulūgh)*

There are three signs of puberty:

1. Fully reaching the age of fifteen, in both males and females;
2. Nocturnal emission[2] (*iḥtilām*) at the age of nine for both males and females, &;
3. Menstruation at the age of nine, in a female.

[2] The intended meaning is the emission of seminal fluid, whether emitted nocturnally or not.

شروط إجزاء الحجر ثمانية. أن يكون بثلاثة أحجار و أن ينقي المحل و أن
لا يجف النجس و أن لا ينتقل و أن لا يطرأ عليه آخر و ألا يجاوز صفحته
و حشفته ولا يصيبه ماء و أن تكون الأحجار طاهرة

Section 3

Section 3: **Bathroom Etiquette** *(istinjā')*

There are eight conditions sufficing the use of stones[3] [or the like, to cleanse oneself after using the bathroom][4]:

1. That three stones are used;[5]
2. That the area be cleansed;[6]
3. That the excreta does not become dry;[7]
4. That the excreta does not move from its place;
5. That the excreta does not mix with a foreign substance;
6. That the excreta does not move from the glans or the anus;
7. That the excreta does not become mixed with water, and;
8. That the stones are pure.[8]

[3] The legal meaning of a 'stone' is a substance that is solid, pure, that has the ability to remove and is not something valued, e.g. not to use a book of knowledge, anything edible or the like, (*Nayl al-Rajā*). Thus tissue paper would suffice.

[4] If any of the eight conditions are not met, the use of water becomes obligatory to cleanse the area.

[5] Meaning no less than three wipes.

[6] Insomuch that the residue could only be removed by water.

[7] To the extent that it could not be removed by a stone, or the like.

[8] Therefore one cannot cleanse oneself, after answering the call to nature, with something that is legally impure.

Section 4: **Ablution** *(wuḍū)*

Section 4/4a فصل فروض الوضوء ستة : الأول النية الثاني غسل الوجه الثالث غسل اليدين مع المرفقين الرابع مسح شئ من الرأس الخامس غسل الرجلين مع الكعبين السادس الترتيب

Section 4 (a): There are six pillars for the ablution:

1. Intention;
2. Washing the face;
3. Washing the arms, including the elbows;
4. Wiping part of the head [with wet hands];
5. Washing the feet, including the ankles, and;
6. The [aforementioned] order.

Section 4b فصل : النية قصد الشيء مقترنا بفعله ومحلها القلب والتلفظ بها سنة ووقتها عند غسل أول جزء من الوجه

Section 4 (b): **Intention** (*niyya*)

Intention is to purpose an act, coinciding with its performance; its place is in the heart, to (audibly) pronounce it is a sunna, and its time enters on washing the first part of the face.[9]

---

9 More specifically the time enters at the beginning of a specific act of worship whose validity is dependent upon ablution.

الترتيب أن لا يقدّم عضو على عضو Section 4c

Section 4 (c): **Order** *(tartīb)*

Order (*tartīb*) [means] not to precede a limb before another limb.[10]

Section 5: **Water Measurements**

فصل : الماء قليل وكثير : القليل ما دون القلتين والكثير قلتان فأكثر القليل
يتنجس بوقوع النجاسة فيه وإن لم يتغير والماء الكثير لا يتنجس إلا إذا تغير Section 5
طعمه أو لونه أو ريحه

Section 5 (a):

Water is [categorised as] a small amount and a large amount. A small amount is less than 216 litres (*qullatain)*, whereas a large amount is 216 litres and above.

Section 5 (b):

A small amount becomes impure if it comes into contact with an impurity, even if its qualities[11] are unaltered;

[10] Meaning an individual would not ordinarily wash the hands and arms until the face is washed.

[11] The qualities being taste, colour and odour.

whereas a large amount of water becomes impure if its taste, colour or odour is altered.

Section 6: **Purificatory Bath** *(ghusl)*

Section 6/6a فصل : موجبات الغسل ستة : إيلاج الحشفة في الفرج وخروج المني
والحيض والنفاس والولادة والموت

Section 6 (a):

There are six things which necessitate the purificatory bath (*ghusl*):

1. The glans penetrating the genitalia;[12]
2. Emission of seminal fluid;
3. Menstruation;
4. Post natal bleeding;
5. Birth, &;
6. Death.[13]

Section 6b فصل : فروض الغسل اثنان : النية وتعميم البدن بالماء

[12] This encompasses the front and rear orifices.
[13] The purificatory bath being an obligation on the umma to fulfil.

Section 6 (b):

There are two pillars for the purificatory bath:

1. Intention, &;
2. For water to flow over the whole body.

فصل شروط الوضوء عشرة : الإسلام و التمييز والنقاء عن الحيض و النفاس وعما يمنع وصول الماء إلى البشرة وأن لا يكون على العضو ما يغير الماء والعلم بفرضيته وأن لا يعتقد فرضاً من فروضه سنة والماء الطهور ودخول الوقت والمولاة لدائم الحدث Section 6c

---

Section 6 (c):

There are ten conditions for ablution (*wuḍū*) [and the purificatory bath]:

1. Islam;
2. Discernment (*tamyīz*);[14]
3. To be free from menstruation and post natal bleeding;
4. [To be free from] that which prevents water reaching the skin;[15]
5. That there be nothing on the limb which results

---

[14] This has numerous definitions and is considered to be in between infancy and puberty. The most common definition is for this individual to be able to eat oneself, drink oneself and wash oneself after answering the call of nature.

[15] Such as dirt or a plaster.

in a change of the water;[16]

6. Knowledge that ablution is obligatory;
7. Not to believe that one of its obligations is a sunna;
8. That the water be purifying;[17]
9. That the time [for prayer] enters, &;
10. Continuation[18] for one continually afflicted with nullifying ones ablution (*dā'im al-ḥadath*).[19]

Section 6d

فصل : نواقض الوضوء أربعة أشياء : الأول الخارج من أحد السبيلين من قبل أو دبر ريح أو غيره إلا المني الثاني زوال العقل بنوم أو غيره إلا نوم قاعد ممكن مقعده من الأرض الثالث إلتقاء بشرتي رجل وامرأة كبيرين أجنبيين من غير حائل الرابع مس قبل الآدمي أو حلقه دبره ببطن الراحة أو بطون الأصابع

Section 6 (d):

Four things nullify the ablution:

1. Anything that exits from the two passages, front or rear, wind or other than [wind], excluding seminal fluid;[20]

---

[16] Such as ink, to the extent that if the water ran over the limb and became the colour of the ink it would no longer be considered water.

[17] As water can be pure, in and of itself, but not purifying. The categorisations of water are dealt with in other books of jurisprudence.

[18] Meaning that there be no long time delay between one's actions of ablution, and between the ablution and prayer.

[19] *Dā'im al-ḥadath* is someone who is continually afflicted with nullifying his ablution, such as the exiting of intermittent drops of urine and the like.

[20] As the emission of seminal fluid necessitates the purificatory bath (ghusl).

2. Loss of cognisance by sleep, or other than [sleep],[21] except sleep in a position firmly seated on the ground;
3. Skin to skin contact, between a male and female, who have reached the age of sexual discrimination, are not from each other's unmarriageable kin (*maḥārim*) and [touch] without a barrier [between them] &;
4. Touching human genitalia, or the anus, with the palm of the hand or the inner parts of the fingers.

فصل : من أنتقض وضوءه حرم عليه أربعة أشياء : الصلاة والطواف ومس المصحف وحمله

Section 6e

Section 6 (e):

Four things are impermissible for one whose ablution is nullified:

1. Prayer;
2. Circumambulation (*ṭawāf*);
3. Touching the Qur'ān &;
4. Carrying the Qur'ān.

[21] Such as losing consciousness, an epileptic fit or intoxication.

Section 6f

ويحرم على الجنب ستة أشياء : الصلاة والطواف ومس المصحف وحمله
واللبث في المسجد و قراءة القران

Section 6 (f):

Six things are impermissible for the one in a state of major ritual impurity (*junub*):

1. Numbers 1 – 4 above;
5. Remaining in the mosque, &;
6. Reciting the Qur'ān.

Section 6g

ويحرم بالحيض عشرة أشياء: الصلاة والطواف ومس المصحف وحمله
واللبث في المسجد وقراءة القران والصوم والطلاق والمرور في المسجد
إن خافت تلويثه والإستمتاع بما بين السرة والركبة

Section 6 (g):

Ten things are impermissible for someone in their menses:

1. Numbers 1 – 6 above;
7. Fasting;
8. Divorce;[22]

[22] It is sinful for a man to divorce his wife whilst she is in her menses, as this prolongs her waiting period *(al-ʿidda)*.

9. Passing through a mosque, if a woman fears soiling it &;
10. [Taking sexual] pleasure from what is between [a woman's] navel and knee.[23]

Section 7: **Earth Ablution** *(tayammum)*

فصل أسباب التيمم ثلاثة : فقد الماء والمرض والإحتياج إليه لعطش حيوان محترم Section 7/7A

Section 7 (a):

Three things allow for the earth ablution (*tayummum*):

1. Loss of water;
2. Illness &;
3. Needing the water for the thirst of an inviolable animal (*ḥayawān muḥtaram*)

غير المحترم ستة : تارك الصلاة والزاني المحصن والمرتد والكافر الحربي والكلب العقور والخنزير Section 7B

---

[23] Without a barrier.

Section 7 (b):

[Those] not inviolable are six:

1. The one who abandons the prayer (*tārik al-ṣalāh*);
2. The married fornicator (*al-zānī al-muḥsin*);
3. The apostate;
4. The warring disbeliever (*al-kāfir al-ḥarbī*);
5. A violent dog &;
6. A pig.

Section 7c

فصل: شروط التيمم عشرة : أن يكون بتراب و أن يكون التراب طاهرا وأن لا يكون مستعملا وأن لا يخالطه دقيق ونحوه وأن يقصده وأن يمسح وجهه ويديه بضربتين وأن يزيل النجاسة أولا وأن يجتهد في القبلة قبله وأن يكون التيمم بعد دخول الوقت وأن يتيمم لكل فرض

Section 7 (c):

There are ten conditions for the earth ablution:

1. To use earth;
2. That the earth be pure;
3. That the earth not be used (*musta'mal*);[24]
4. That the earth has not been mixed with flour or the like;

[24] Used earth is that which remains on the limb (from the earth ablution), or the excess earth that falls from the limb.

5. That one intends use of the earth;
6. That one wipes one's face and hands with two strikes;
7. That any impurity is removed prior to making the earth ablution;
8. That one endeavours to judge the direction of the qibla beforehand;[25]
9. That the earth ablution occur after the time [for prayer] has entered &;
10. That one performs the earth ablution for every obligatory act of worship.

فصل فروض التيمم خمسة: الأول نقل التراب الثاني النية الثالث مسح
الوجه الرابع مسح اليدين مع المرفقين الخامس الترتيب بين المسحتين Section 7d

---

Section 7 (d):

There are five pillars for the earth ablution:

1. Transferring the earth;
2. Intention;
3. Wiping the face;
4. Wiping the arms including the elbows &;
5. Order between the two wipes.

[25] This condition is stipulated by Ibn Ḥajar al-Haitamī. Imam al-Ramlī does not hold this to be a condition.

Section 7e

فصل مبطلات التيمّم ثلاثة : ما أبطل الوضوء والردة وتوهم الماء إن تيمم لفقده

Section 7 (e):

Three things nullify the earth ablution:

1. That which nullifies the ablution (as mentioned in section 6 (a) 1-4);
2. Apostasy, &;
3. Suspecting that water is present, if one performed the earth ablution due to loss of it.

Section 8/8a

فصل : الذي يطهر من النجاسات ثلاثة : الخمر إذا تخللت بنفسها وجلد الميتة إذا دبغ و ما صار حيواناً

Section 8: **Impurities Transformed**

Section 8 (a)

Three things are purified from being (inherently) impure:

1. Wine, if it independently transforms into vinegar;
2. The hide of a dead animal, if tanned, &;
3. That which metamorphosed into a life form.[26]

[26] Such as maggots emanating from a dead carcass.

Section 9: **Impurities** *(najāsāt)*

فصل النجاسات ثلاث : مغلظة ومخففة ومتوسطة . المغلظة نجاسة الكلب والخنزير وفرع أحدهما والمخففة بول الصبي الذي لم يطعم غير اللبن ولم يبلغ الحولين والمتوسطة سائر النجاسات Section 9/9a

---

Section 9 (a):

There are three impurities:

1. Heavy impurity;
2. Light impurity, &;
3. Intermediate impurity.

    1. Heavy impurity is the impurity of a dog, a pig, or the offspring of either of the two.
    2. Light impurity is the urine of a male infant, who has only been fed [breast] milk, and has yet to reach the age of two, &;
    3. Intermediate impurity is the remainder of impurities.

Section 9B/9C/9D

فصل : المغلظة تطهر بسبع غسلات بعد إزالة عينها إحداهن بتراب والمخففة تطهر برش الماء عليها مع الغلبة وإزالة عينها والمتوسطة تنقسم على قسمين : عينية وحكمية العينية التي لها لون وريح وطعم فلا بد من إزالة لونها وريحها وطعمها والحكمية التي لا لون ولا ريح ولا طعم لها يكفيك جري الماء عليها

Section 9 (b):

Heavy impurity is cleansed by seven washes after removing the core of the impurity, one of the washes being with earth [mixed with water].

Section 9 (c):

Light impurity is cleansed by sprinkling water upon the impurity after removing the core of it.

Section 9 (d):

Intermediate impurity is divided into two types:

1. Discernible impurity *('ainiyya)* &;
2. Indiscernible impurity *(ḥukmiyya)*

As for discernible impurity it is that which has a colour, odour and taste; thus removal of these three traits is obligatory.

As for indiscernible impurity it is that which has none of the above [traits] thus it suffices to run water over it.[27]

Section 10: **Menstruation** *(ḥaiḍ)*

فصل : أقل الحيض يوم وليلة وغالبه ست أو سبع وأكثره خمسة عشرة يوما بلياليها أقل الطهر بين الحيضتين خمسة عشر يوما وغالبه أربعة و عشرون يوما أو ثلاثة و عشرون يوما و لا حد لأكثره أقل النفاس مجة و غالبه أربعون يوماً وأكثره ستون يوما

Section 10/10a/10b

Section 10 (a)

The minimum menstruation period is twenty-four hours, whilst six or seven days is the norm, and the maximum (legal) period is fifteen days including nights.

The minimum purity cycle[28] between two menses is fifteen days; the norm is twenty-three or twenty-four days whilst the maximum (legal) period has no defined limit.

Section 10 (b)

The minimum postnatal bleeding period is momentary, whilst forty days is the norm, and the maximum (legal) period is sixty days.

---

[27] Such as urine afflicting ones clothes and after drying has neither odour nor colour.

[28] A purity cycle is the interval between two menses.

THE BOOK OF PRAYER

فصل أعذار الصلاة اثنان : النوم و النسيان Section 11/11A

Section 11: **Excuses for Missing Prayer**

Section 11 (a)

There are two excuses for [missing] prayer:

1. Sleep &;
2. Forgetfulness.

فصل : شروط الصلاة ثمانية : طهارة الحدثين والطهارة عن النجاسة في الثوب
والبدن والمكان وستر العورة و إستقبال القبلة ودخول الوقت والعلم بفرضيتها Section 12/12A
وأن لا يعتقد فرضاً من فروضها سنة و إجتناب المبطلات

SECTION 12: **Prayer Conditions**

SECTION 12 (A)

There are eight conditions for prayer:[29]

1. Purity from minor and major ritual impurity;
2. Purity from filth in one's clothes, body and place [of prayer];
3. Covering one's nakedness (*'aura*);
4. Facing the qibla;
5. That the time [for prayer] enters;
6. Knowledge of the obligation of prayer;
7. Not to believe that a pillar of the prayer is a sunna, &;
8. Abstaining from that which invalidates the prayer.

SECTION 13: **Ritual Impurities** *(aḥdāth)*

الأحداث إثنان : أصغر وأكبر فالأصغر ما أوجب الوضوء والأكبر ما أوجب الغسل

SECTION 13 (A)

There are two ritual impurities:

1. Minor, &;
2. Major.

[29] These are the conditions in order for prayer to be 'valid' (*ṣaḥīh*) and not the conditions for whom the prayer is obligatory upon.

Minor is that which necessitates ablution (*wuḍū*), and major is that which necessitates the purificatory bath (*ghusl*)

Section 14: **Nakedness** *(ʿaura)*

العورات أربع : عورة الرجل مطلقا (والأمة في الصلاة) ما بين السرة والركبة
وعورة الحرة في الصلاة جميع بدنها ما سوى الوجه والكفين وعورة الحرة (والأمة) Section 14/14A
عند الأجانب جميع البدن (وعند محارمها والنساء ما بين السرة والركبة) .

Section 14 (a)

There are three types of nakedness (ʿ*aura*):

1. The nakedness of a man, whether in or out of prayer, is between the navel and the knee;
2. The nakedness of a woman, in prayer, is her whole body except the face and hands;
3. The nakedness of a woman, in the company of strangers,[30] is the entire body;

Section 15: **Pillars of Prayer**

فصل : أركان الصلاة سبعة عشر : الأول النية الثاني تكبيرة الإحرام الثالث
القيام على القادر في الفرض الرابع قراءة الفاتحة الخامس الركوع السادس Section 15/15A

[30] These being other than their unmarriageable kin (*maḥārim*)

الطمأنينة فيه السابع الإعتدال الثامن الطمأنينة فيه التاسع السجود مرتين
TION 15A العاشر الطمأنينة فيه الحادي عشر الجلوس بين السجدتين الثاني عشر
الطمأنينة فيه الثالث عشر التشهد الأخير الرابع عشر القعود فيه الخامس
عشر الصلاة على النبي صلى الله عليه وسلم فيه السادس عشر السلام
السابع عشر الترتيب

Section 15 (a)

There are seventeen pillars of prayer:

1. Intention;
2. The opening '*Allahu Akbar*';
3. Standing for one who is able, in an obligatory prayer;
4. Reciting the Fātiḥa;
5. Bowing (*rukū'*);
6. Remaining still therein;
7. Straightening up (*'itidāl*);
8. Remaining still therein;
9. Prostrating twice;
10. Remaining still therein;
11. Sitting between the two prostrations;
12. Remaining still therein;
13. The last tashahhud;
14. Sitting in the last tashahhud;
15. Sending prayers upon the Prophet ﷺ therein;
16. Saying '*al-salām 'alaikum*' (*taslīm*);
17. The [aforementioned] order.

Section 16: **Intention** *(niyya)*

فصل : النية ثلاث درجات إن كانت الصلاة فرضاً وجب قصد الفعل
والتعيين والفرضية وإن كانت نافلة مؤقتة كراتبة أو ذات سبب وجب قصد Section
الفعل والتعيين وإن كانت نافلة مطلقة وجب قصد الفعل فقط الفعل أصلي 16/16a
والتعيين ظهراً أو عصراً والفرضية فرضاً

Section 16 (a)

Intention is three levels:

1. One must intend to pray, specify the prayer and state that it is obligatory, if the prayer is obligatory [such as *maghrib*];

2. One must intend to pray and specify the prayer, if the prayer is a designated supererogatory prayer (*rātiba*), such as the sunna prayers which precede and follow the obligatory prayers; or a prayer based on a (specific) cause [like the rain prayer];

3. One must simply intend to pray, if the prayer is supererogatory.

   Intention to pray is [to state] 'I pray.' Specification is *ẓuhr* or '*asr,* [for instance]. Stating that it is obligatory is [to say] 'obligatory.'[31]

[31] Thus it would suffice to intend to say 'I pray the obligatory fajr prayer' for example.

Section 17: **Conditions of the Opening Allahu Akbar**

فصل شروط تكبيرة الإحرام ستة عشر: أن تقع حالة القيام في الفرض وأن تكون بالعربية وأن تكون بلفظ الجلالة وبلفظ أكبر والترتيب بين اللفظين وأن لا يمد همزة الجلالة وعدم مد باء أكبر وأن لا يشدد الباء وأن لا يزيد واواً ساكنة أو متحركة بين الكلمتين وأن لا يزيد واواً قبل الجلالة وأن لا يقف بين كلمتي التكبير وقفة طويلة ولا قصيرة وأن يسمع نفسه جميع حروفها ودخول الوقت في المؤقت وإيقاعها حال الإستقبال وأن لا يخل بحرف من حروفها وتأخير تكبيرة المأموم عن تكبيرة الإمام

Section 17 (a)

There are sixteen conditions for the opening '*Allahu Akbar*':

1. To occur whilst standing in an obligatory prayer;
2. To be in Arabic;
3 To be phrased using the word(s) 'Allah';
4. And the word 'Akbar';
5. Order between the two words;
6. Not to elongate the letter 'hamza' ا [which equates to the 'a'] in the word Allah;
7. Not to elongate the letter 'bā' ب [which equates to the 'b'] in the word Akbar;

8. Not to emphasise the letter 'bā' ب ('b') in the word Akbar;
9. Not to add a 'waw' و with or without a vowel marking between the two words;
10. Not to add a 'waw' و before the word Allah;
11. Not to pause between the two words;
12. For one to hear all the letters [pronounced];
13. For the time of prayer to enter for prayer dependent upon this;[32]
14. To occur whilst facing the qibla;
15. Not to violate [pronunciation of] the letters, &;
16. For the follower to delay his 'Allahu Akbar' till after the imam's.

SECTION 18: **Conditions of the Fātiḥa**

فصل : شروط الفاتحة عشرة : الترتيب والمولاة ومراعاة حروفها ومراعاة
تشديداتها وأن لا يسكت سكتة طويلة ولا قصيرة يقصد بها قطع القراءة
وقراءة كل آياتها ومنها البسملة وعدم اللحن المخل بالمعنى وأن تكون حالة SECTION 18/18A
القيام في الفرض وأن يسمع نفسه القراءة وأن لا يتخللها ذكر أجنبي

---

32 Meaning dependant upon the time entering e.g. maghrib as opposed to a supererogatory prayer.

SECTION 18 (A)

There are ten conditions for the Fātiḥa:

1. Order;[33]
2. Continuation;
3. Paying attention to the letters;
4. Paying attention to the emphases;[34]
5. Not to commit a long or short pause intending to cease reciting;[35]
6. Reciting all the verses, from them being the '*Bismillah al-Raḥmān al-Raḥīm*';
7. Not to recite in a manner that alters the meaning;
8. To occur whilst standing in an obligatory prayer;[36]
9. To ensure the reciter hears the recitation, &;
10. Not to breach the recitation with an invocation (*dhikr*) that one is not commanded to recite.

ION 18B

فصل: تشديدات الفاتحة أربع عشرة : بسم الله فوق اللام الرحمن فوق
الراء الرحيم فوق الراء الحمد لله فوق لام الجلالة رب العالمين فوق الباء
الرحمن فوق الراء الرحيم فوق الراء مالك يوم الدين فوق الدال إياك نعبد
فوق الياء وإياك نستعين فوق الياء اهدنا الصراط المستقيم فوق الصاد

---

33 Meaning not to change the order of the verses of the Fātiḥa

34 Meaning that the rules of tajwīd are not violated.

35 If one committed a long pause the recitation of the Fātiḥa would be nullified, whether one intended to cease or not, thus the 'intention to cease' is related to a short pause. A long pause equates to the duration it takes to inhale and exhale, and a short pause is less than this.

36 As standing is not obligatory in a supererogatory prayer, hence in a non-obligatory prayer one could recite it in the sitting position.

صراط الذين فوق اللام أنعمت عليهم غير المغضوب عليهم و لا الضآلين فوق الضاد و اللام Section

---

Section 18 (b):

The Fātiḥa has fourteen emphases [refer to the original Arabic text of *Safīnat al-Najā* above].

فصل : يسن رفع اليدين في أربعة مواضع : عند تكبيرة الإحرام وعند الركوع وعند الإعتدال وعند القيام من التشهد الأول Section 19/19a

---

Section 19: **Raising Hands in Prayer**

Section 19 (a)

It is sunna to raise one's hands in four places:

1. Upon the opening 'Allahu Akbar';
2. Upon bowing (*rukū'*);
3. Upon straightening up (*'itidāl*), &;
4. Upon standing after the first tashahhud.

Section 20: **Conditions for Prostration**

فصل : شروط السجود سبعة : أن يسجد على سبعة أعضاء وأن تكون جبهته مكشوفة والتحامل برأسه وعدم الهوي لغيره وأن لا يسجد على شيء يتحرك بحركته وإرتفاع أسافله على أعاليه والطمأنينة فيه Section 20/20a

SECTION 20 (A)

There are seven conditions for prostration:

1. To prostrate upon seven limbs;
2. For one's forehead to be uncovered;
3. To apply slight pressure with one's head, to the ground;
4. Not to move into prostration for an external reason;
5. Not to prostrate on something that moves with one's movement;
6. To raise the posterior and hips above the shoulders and head, &;
7. To remain motionless therein.

ION 20B

خاتمة : أعضاء السجود سبعة : الجبهة وبطون الكفين والركبتان وبطون أصابع الرجلين

SECTION 20 (B):

There are seven limbs of prostration:

1. The forehead;
2 & 3. The insides of both hands;
4 & 5. Both knees, &;
6 & 7. The insides of the toes of both feet.

فصل : تشديدات التشهد إحدى وعشرون : خمس في أكمله وستة عشر في أقله التحيات على التاء والياء المباركات الصلوات على الصاد الطيبات على الطاء والياء لله على لام الجلالة السلام على السين عليك أيها النبي على الياء والنون والياء ورحمة الله على لام الجلالة وبركاته السلام على السين علينا وعلى عباد الله على لام الجلالة الصالحين على الصاد أشهد أن لا إله على لام ألف إلا الله على لام ألف ولام الجلالة وأشهد أن على النون محمدا رسول الله على ميم محمد وعلى الراء وعلى لام الجلالة فصل : تشديدات أقل الصلاة على النبي أربع : اللهم على اللام والميم صل على اللام على محمد على الميم فصل: أقل السلام السلام عليكم تشديد السلام على السين Section 21/21a

Section 21: **Emphases**

Section 21 (a)

There are twenty-one emphases in the tashahhud, four in prayers upon the Prophet ﷺ and one in the salām [refer to the original text of *Safīnat al-Najā* above]

Section 22: **Prayer Times**

فصل : أوقات الصلاة خمس : أول وقت الظهر زوال الشمس وآخره مصير ظل الشيء مثله غير ظل الإستواء وأول وقت العصر إذا صار ظل كل شيء مثله و زاد قليلاً وآخره غروب الشمس وأول وقت المغرب Section 22/22a

غروب الشمس وآخره غروب الشفق الأحمر وأول وقت العشاء غروب
الشفق الأحمر وآخره طلوع الفجر الصادق وأول وقت الصبح طلوع الفجر TION 22A
الصادق وآخره طلوع الشمس

Section 22 (a)

There are five prayer times:

1. The midday prayer (*ẓuhr*) commences with the sun declining from the zenith, and concludes with the shadow reaching its equivalent in length, excluding the shadow of the zenith;
2. The mid-afternoon prayer (*ʿaṣr*) commences when the shadow of something equals its length with a slight addition, and concludes with sunset;
3. The sunset prayer (*maghrib*) commences with the setting of the sun, and concludes with the eclipse of the twilight [i.e. redness of the sky];
4. The night-time prayer (*ʿishāʾ*) commences with the eclipse of the twilight, and concludes with the emergence of true dawn;[37]
5. The dawn prayer (*ṣubḥ*) commences with true dawn, and concludes with sunrise.

---

37 True dawn *(fajr al-ṣādiq)* is defined as an incremental light emerging across the horizon moving northward.

الأشفاق الثلاثة : أحمر وأصفر وأبيض الأحمر مغرب والأصفر والأبيض عشاء ويندب تأخير صلاة العشاء إلى أن يغيب الشفق الأصفر والأبيض SECTION

SECTION 22 (B):

There are three twilights; red, yellow and white. Red equates to the sunset prayer, and yellow and white equate to the night-time prayer. It is recommended to defer the night-time prayer until the yellow and white twilights fade away.

فصل : تحرم الصلاة التي ليس لها سبب متقدم ولا مقارن في خمسة أوقات : عند طلوع الشمس حتى ترتفع قدر رمح وعند الإستواء في غير يوم الجمعة حتى تزول وعند الإصفرار حتى تغرب وبعد صلاة الصبح حتى تطلع الشمس وبعد صلاة العصر حتى تغرب SECTION

SECTION 22 (C):

It is impermissible to pray a prayer, that has no preceding reason, nor a coinciding reason [such as the eclipse prayer] at five times:

1. At sunrise, until the sun rises [above the horizon] the measure of a spear's length;[38]

[38] This equates to 336 cm in height *(sabaʿ adhruʿ)*

2. At the zenith, until it subsides, excluding Friday;
3. At the sun's yellowness (*iṣfirār*), [between mid-afternoon and sunset] until sunset;
4. After the dawn prayer (*ṣubḥ*), until the sun rises;
5. After the mid-afternoon prayer (*'aṣr*), until the sun sets.

Section 23: **Pauses**

فصل : سكتات الصلاة ستة : بين تكبيرة الإحرام ودعاء الإفتتاح وبين دعاء الإفتتاح والتعوذ وبين الفاتحة والتعوذ وبين آخر الفاتحة وآمين و بين آمين والسورة وبين السورة والركوع

Section 23 (a)

There are six pauses in the prayer[39] (*sakatāt al-ṣalāh*):

1. Between the opening 'Allahu Akbar' and the opening supplication (*iftitāḥ*);
2. Between the opening supplication (*iftitāḥ*) and the ta'wwudh [seeking refuge];
3. Between the Fātiḥa and the ta'wwudh;
4. Between the end of the Fātiḥa and saying āmīn;
5. Between saying āmīn and the chapter (of Qur'ān);
6. Between the chapter (of Qur'ān) and bowing (*rukū'*).

---

[39] A pause equals the duration of saying '*Subḥān Allah*'.

فصل : الأركان التي تلزمه فيها الطمأنينة أربعة : الركوع والإعتدال و السجود والجلوس بين السجدتين SECTION 24/24A

SECTION 24: **Stillness** *(ṭuma'nīna)*

SECTION 24 (A)

There are four pillars that necessitate stillness (*ṭuma'nīna*) [defined below]:

1. Bowing (*rukū'*);
2. Straightening up (*'itidāl*);
3. Prostration &;
4. Sitting between the two prostrations.

الطمأنينة هي : سكون بعد حركة بحيث يستقر كل عضو محله بقدر سبحان الله SECTION

SECTION 24 (B):

Stillness (*ṭuma'nīna*) is [defined as], 'composure after movement, whereby one's limbs remain motionless in their place for the duration of [saying] '*Subḥān Allah*'

Section 25: **Prostrating Out of Absentmindedness**

فصل : أسباب سجود السهو أربعة : الأول ترك بعض من أبعاض الصلاة أو
بعض البعض الثاني فعل ما يبطل عمده ولا يبطل سهوه إذا فعله ناسياً الثالث
نقل ركن قولي إلى غير محله الرابع إيقاع ركن فعلي مع إحتمال الزيادة

Section 25 (a):

There are four causes to prostrate out of absentmindedness:

1. Leaving all, or part of, a principal sunna[40] (*ba'ḍ*), from the principal sunnas of prayer (see section 26);
2. An action that would invalidate the prayer if done so intentionally, but not if done absentmindedly,[41] out of forgetfulness.
3. Committing a vocal pillar in an incorrect place[42], &;
4. Performing a motion pillar, with the possibility of it being additional.

---

[40] A principal sunna is a sunna that necessitates the prostration of absentmindedness (*sujūd al-sahu*) if omitted.

[41] Such as absentmindedly speaking a small amount, which would ordinarily invalidate the prayer if done so intentionally.

[42] Such as reciting the Fātiḥa whilst bowing.

فصل أبعاض الصلاة سبعة : التشهد الأول وقعوده والصلاة على النبي
صلى الله عليه وسلم فيه والصلاة على الآل في التشهد الأخير والقنوت SECTION 26/26A
والصلاة والسلام على النبي صلى الله عليه وسلم وآله وصحبه فيه

SECTION 26: **Principal Sunnas** *(ab'āḍ)*

SECTION 26 (A):

There are seven Principal Sunnas for prayer:

1. The first tashahhud;
2. Sitting therein;
3. Sending prayer upon the Prophet ﷺ therein;
4. Sending prayer upon his Family in the last tashahhud;
5. The supplication in the dawn prayer (*qunūt*);
6. Standing therein &;
7. Sending prayer upon the Prophet ﷺ, his Family and Companions therein.

SECTION 27: **Invalidation of Prayer**

فصل : تبطل الصلاة بأربع عشرة خصلة : بالحدث وبوقوع النجاسة إن
لم تلق حالاً من غير حمل وإنكشاف العورة إن لم تستر حالاً والنطق SECTION 27/27A
بحرفين أو حرف مفهم عمداً و بالمفطر عمداً والأكل الكثير ناسيا وثلاث
حركات متواليات ولو سهواً والوثبة الفاحشة والضربة المفرطة وزيادة

ركن فعلي عمداً والتقدم على إمامه بركنين فعليين والتخلف بهما بغير عذر
:ION 27A
ونية قطع الصلاة وتعليق قطعها بشيء والتردد في قطعها

SECTION 27 (A):

Fourteen things invalidate the prayer:

1. [Minor or major] ritual impurity;
2. Filth being on one's person, if not discarded immediately, without carrying it;
3. Exposing one's nakedness, unless covered immediately;
4. Intentionally vocalising two letters, or one meaningful letter;[43]
5. Committing that which invalidates one's fasting;
6. Excessive eating, if done so forgetfully;[44]
7. Three consecutive movements, even if committed absentmindedly;
8. An excessive jump;
9. An excessive hit;[45]
10. Intentionally adding a motion pillar;[46]
11. Preceding the imam, or trailing behind him, by two motion pillars, without a [valid] excuse;[47]

---

[43] A meaningful letter, refers to specific letters in Arabic that express meaning, such as عِ meaning 'pay attention' or قِ meaning 'protect'.

[44] Eating more than a sesame seed delineates this, although certain scholars mention a morsel. Thus if done so intentionally, one's prayer would be invalidated.

[45] Numbers 8 & 9 refer to a movement involving the whole body.

[46] Such as an additional prostration; thus this excludes a vocal pillar, such as reciting the Fatiha, which necessitates the prostration of absent-mindedness as previously mentioned.

[47] Valid excuses for leading the imam are forgetfulness and ignorance of

12. Intention to break the prayer;
13. Making one's intention to break the prayer contingent upon something,[48] &;
14. Hesitating in intending to break one's prayer.

Section 28: **Intention for Leading Prayer**

فصل الذي يلزم فيه نية الإمامة أربع : الجمعة والمعادة والمنذورة جماعةً والمتقدمة في المطر Section 28/28a

---

Section 28 (a):

There are four instances where the intention to lead the prayer are necessary:

1. Friday prayer (*jumua'*);
2. Repeating prayer in congregation;
3. A prayer sworn to be prayed in congregation, &;
4. The first of two prayers combined due to rain.

Section 29: **Conditions for Following the Imam**

فصل : شروط القدوة أحد عشر: أن لا يعلم بطلان صلاة إمامه بحدث أو غيره وأن لا يعتقد وجوب قضائها عليه وأن لا يكون مأموماً ولا أمياً وأن Section 29/29a

---

the legal ruling, as for trailing the imam, from amongst the excuses, are being slow in reciting the Fātiha or the like.

[48] Such as 'if so and so knocks on my door I will cease to pray'.

ION 29A

لا يتقدم عليه في الموقف وأن يعلم إنتقالات إمامه وأن يجتمعا في مسجد أو
ثلاثة مائة ذراع تقريبا وأن ينوي القدوة أو الجماعة وأن يتوافق نظم صلاتهما
وأن لا يخالفه في سنة فاحشة مخالفة وأن يتابعه

Section 29 (a)

There are eleven conditions for following the imam [in prayer]:

1. That one does not believe the imam's prayer to be invalid, based on minor or major ritual impurity or other than this;[49]
2. To not believe that the imam has to make up the prayer he is praying;
3. That the imam is not a follower;
4. That the imam can correctly recite the Fātiḥa;
5. Not to be in front of one's imam;
6. To know the movements of the imam; [50]
7. To congregate in a mosque, or in the vicinity of 144 metres (approximately);
8. To intend to follow, or (pray in) congregation;
9. That there is conformity between the prayer of the imam and the follower(s);[51]

---

[49] Such as following an imam whilst believing him to be facing the wrong direction.

[50] Meaning when the imam moves from standing to bowing to prostrating etc.

[51] Thus if the imam was praying the funeral prayer and the followers were praying ẓuhr, for instance, this would be considered invalid.

10. Not to openly oppose one's imam in a sunna;[52] &
11. To follow the imam.

فصل : صور القدوة تسع : تصح في خمس : قدوة رجل برجل قدوة امرأة
برجل وقدوة خنثى برجل وقدوة امرأة بخنثى وقدوة امرأة بامرأة وتبطل
في أربع : قدوة رجل بامرأة وقدوة رجل بخنثى وقدوة خنثى بامرأة وقدوة
خنثى بخنثى

SECTION 29 (B):

There are nine scenarios in following the imam:

They are valid in five instances:

1. A man following a man;
2. A woman following a man;
3. A hermaphrodite following a man;
4. A woman following a hermaphrodite, &;
5. A woman following a woman.

And invalid in four instances:

1. A man following a woman;
2. A man following a hermaphrodite;
3. A hermaphrodite following a woman, &;
4. A hermaphrodite following a hermaphrodite.

---

[52] Such as the imam prostrating on reciting a verse of prostration, and the congregation not following him into this prostration.

Section 30: **Joining Prayers**

فصل شروط جمع التقديم أربعة : البداءة بالأولى ونية الجمع فيها والمولاة بينهما ودوام العذر

Section 30 (a):

There are four conditions for joining 'aṣr with ẓuhr or 'ishā' with maghrib (*jama' taqdīm*):

1. To begin with the first of the two prayers;
2. That the intention to join occur in the first of the two prayers;
3. Continuation between the two prayers,[53] &;
4. That the dispensation continues (until the end of the prayer(s)).

فصل : شروط جمع التأخير إثنان : نية التأخير وقد بقي من وقت الأولى ما يسعها ودوام العذر إلى تمام الثانية

Section 30 (b):

There are two conditions for delaying ẓuhr till 'aṣr and maghrib till 'ishā' (*jama' ta'khīr*);

---

53 This is delineated by a gap the duration of two light *raka's*; thus one must not delay between the two prayers longer than this.

1. Intending to delay [the prayer] whilst time remains[54] to encompass the first of the two prayers, &;
2. That the dispensation continues until the end of the second of the two prayers.

SECTION 31: **Shortening Prayer** (*qaṣr*)

فصل شروط القصر سبعة : أن يكون سفره مرحلتين وأن يكون مباحا
والعلم بجواز القصر ونية القصر عند الإحرام وأن تكون الصلاة رباعية SECTION 31/31A
ودوام السفر إلى تمامها وأن لا يقتدي بمتم في جزء من صلاته

SECTION 31 (A)

There are seven conditions for shortening the prayer:

1. That the journey is (at least) 81 kilometres [approximately]or more;
2. That the journey is lawful;[55]
3. That one has knowledge of the permissibility to shorten the prayer;
4. That one intends to shorten [the prayer] upon making the opening '*Allahu Akbar*';
5. That the prayer consists of four units (*raka'*);[56]
6. That the journey continues until the end of the prayer(s), &;

---

[54] Meaning the time of the first of the two prayers remains.

[55] Meaning one does not travel for a sinful purpose or the like.

[56] Thus there is no shortening the maghrib or fajr prayers.

7. That one does not follow someone who is completing the full prayer, in any part of one's prayer.

SECTION 32: **The Friday Prayer** *(jumua‘)*

فصل شروط الجمعة ستة : أن تكون كلها في وقت الظهر وأن تقام في خطة البلد و أن تصلى جماعة و أن يكونوا أربعين أحرارا ذكوراً بالغين مستوطنين و أن لا تسبقها ولا تقارنها جمعة في تلك البلد و أن يتقدمها خطبتان

SECTION 32 (A)

There are six conditions for the Friday prayer (*jumua‘*):

1. That it takes place during the time of the midday prayer (*ẓuhr*);
2. That it takes place in a town;[57]
3. That it be prayed in congregation;
4. That it be performed by forty pubescent males, who are residents;[58]
5. That the prayer is not preceded by another Friday prayer, nor prayed in conjunction with one, in that town, &;
6. That the prayer is preceded by two sermons.

---

57 Thus not being obligatory on one residing in the desert, or uninhabited locality.

58 Defined as one who is not a traveller, nor travels from one's place of residence, except for a valid need.

فصل أركان الخطبتين خمسة : حمد الله فيهما والصلاة على النبي صلى الله عليه وسلم فيهما والوصية بالتقوى فيهما وقراءة آية من القرآن في إحداهما والدعاء للمؤمنين والمؤمنات في الأخيرة

SECTION

SECTION 32 (B):

There are five pillars for the two sermons:

1. To say '*al-ḥamduliLlah*' in both sermons;
2. To send prayer upon the Prophet ﷺ in both;
3. To counsel to fear God, also in both;
4. To read a verse (*āyah*) of the Qur'ān in one of the sermons,[59] &;
5. To supplicate for the believers in the last sermon.

فصل شروط الخطبتين عشرة: الطهارة عن الحدثين الأصغر والأكبر والطهارة عن النجاسة في الثوب والبدن والمكان وستر العورة والقيام على القادر والجلوس بينهما فوق طمأنينة الصلاة والموالاة بينهما والموالاة بينهما وبين الصلاة وأن تكون بالعربية وأن يسمعها أربعون وأن تكون كلها في وقت الظهر

SECTION

[59] Preferably at the end of the first sermon.

Section 32 (c):

There are ten conditions for the two sermons:

1. To be free of minor or major ritual impurity;
2. To be free of impurity in one's clothes, body and place;
3. To cover one's nakedness;
4. To stand for one who is able;
5. To sit between the two sermons for the duration of saying '*Subḥan Allah*';
6. Continuation between the two sermons;
7. Continuation between the two sermons and the prayer;
8. That they are in Arabic;
9. That the sermon is audible to forty attendees, &;
10. That they are performed during the time of the midday prayer (*ẓuhr*).

THE BOOK OF FUNERAL LAW

فصل : الذي يلزم للميت أربع خصال : غسله وتكفينه والصلاة عليه ودفنه

SECTION 33/33A

SECTION 33: **That Which is Necessary for the Deceased**

SECTION 33 (A):

There are four things necessary for the deceased:

1. Washing the deceased;
2. Shrouding the deceased (*takfīn*);
3. Praying over the deceased, &;
4. Burying the deceased.

SECTION 33 (B): **Washing**

فصل : أقل الغسل تعميم بدنه بالماء و أكمله أن يغسل سوأتيه و أن يزيل القذر من أنفه و أن يوضئه و أن يدلك بالسدر و أن يصب الماء عليه ثلاثاً

SECTION

The minimum acceptable washing is for water to flow over the whole body. The optimal method is to wash the private parts, then to remove any waste matter from the nose, to perform ablution for the deceased, to rub the body with zizyphus spina christi; lotus tree (*sidr*), and then to pour water over the body thrice.

Section 33 (c): **Shrouding**

'ION 33C فصل : أقل الكفن ثوب يعمه وأكمله للرجل ثلاث لفائف وللمراءة قميص
وخمار وإزار ولفافتان

The minimum shroud is a cloth that would cover the body; the optimal, for a male is to use three separate cloths. And for a female, an upper garment, a head cover, a wrap and two cloths.

Section 33 (d): **Prayer**

'ION 33D فصل أركان صلاة الجنازة سبعة : الأول النية الثاني أربع تكبيرات الثالث
القيام على القادر الرابع قراءة الفاتحة الخامس الصلاة على النبي صلى الله
عليه وسلم بعد الثانية السادس الدعاء للميت بعد الثالثة السابع السلام

There are seven pillars for the funeral prayer:

1. Intention;
2. Four *takbīrs* [saying Allahu Akbar];
3. Standing for one who is able;
4. Reciting the Fātiḥa;
5. Prayer upon the Prophet ﷺ, after the second Allahu Akbar;
6. Supplication for the deceased, after the third Allahu Akbar, &;
7. Saying 'al-salām 'alaikum' (*taslīm*).

Section 33 (e): **Burial**

فصل : أقل الدفن حفرة تكتم رائحته وتحرسه من السباع وأكمله قامة
وبسطه ويوضع خده على التراب ويجب توجيهه إلى القبلة

The minimum size of the grave is an opening that would conceal the odour of the deceased, and safeguard him from predatory animals.

The optimal method is [for the opening] to equal his height, if arms outstretched, and to place his cheek on the earth. It is obligatory to direct him towards the qibla.

فصل : ينبش الميت لأربع خصال : للغسل إذا لم يتغير ولتوجيهه إلى القبلة
وللمال إذا دفن معه وللمرأة إذا دفن جنينها معها وأمكنت حياته

SECTION 33 (F):

Exhuming the deceased is obligatory in four instances:

1. To wash [the body, if not washed] as long as the body has not altered;[60]
2. To direct the body towards the qibla;
3. For [acquisition of] wealth, if buried with the body, &;
4. [To exhume] a woman, if buried with her foetus, if the possibility of life [for the foetus] exists.

فصل : الإستعانات أربع خصال: مباحة وخلاف الأولى ومكروهة
وواجبة فالمباحة هي تقريب الماء وخلاف الأولى هي صب الماء على
نحو المتوضئ والمكروهة هي لمن يغتسل أعضاءه والواجبة هي للمريض
عند العجز

SECTION 34: **Seeking Assistance** *(isti'ānāt)*

SECTION 34 (A):

Seeking assistance is of four types:

1. Permissible (*mubāḥa*);
2. Contrary to what is better (*khilāf al-aula*);
3. Disliked (*mukrūha*), &;
4. Obligatory (*wājiba*).

---

60 Meaning begun to decompose.

1. As for 'permissible' [an example of] this is to bring water [for someone else to perform ablution].

2. 'Contrary to what is better' is e.g. pouring water for someone who is performing ablution.

3. 'Disliked' is when one washes somone else's limbs (during the ablution, without excuse).

4. 'Obligatory' is for [helping] someone ill, when [they are] unable [to do so independently].

THE BOOK OF ZAKĀT

فصل الأموال التي تلزم فيها الزكاة ستة أنواع : النعم والنقدان والمعشرات
وأموال التجارة واجبها ربع عشر قيمة عروض التجارة والركاز والمعدن

Section 35: **Zakāt Categories**

Section 35 (a):

Wealth that requires one to pay zakāt on is of six types:

1. Livestock (*na'm*);
2. Goldandsilver [includingmonetaryequivalent(s)] (*naqdān*);
3. Food Crops (*mu'ash-sharāt*);
4. Trade Merchandise [zakāt being 2.5 percent on the value of the merchandise] (*'urūḍ al-tijāra);*
5. Mined gold and silver (*m'adin*) &;
6. Buried gold and silver (*rikāz*).

The original text of *Safīnat al-Najā* concludes here. The following are points summarised for each category but do not constitute the original text.

Livestock *(an'ām)*

Section 35 (b):

Livestock equates to camels, cattle and goats only. Thus in the school of Imam al-Shāfi'ī zakāt is not obligatory for one who owns horses and the like.

Section 35 (c):

Zakāt is obligatory on livestock once three conditions are fulfilled:

1. That a lunar year elapses and the owner is in full possession of the livestock;
2. That the livestock have been grazed on unowned open range pasture, &;
3. That the livestock constitute the 'minimum zakāt payable amount' (*niṣāb*) or above.

Section 35 (d)

The minimum zakāt payable amount (*niṣāb*):

For camels the number is five, for cattle, thirty and for goats, forty. Thus there is no zakāt to be paid by an owner who owns less than the 'minimum zakāt payable amount'. The amount payable is expounded upon in the books of jurisprudence.

Gold & Silver *(naqdān)* [and their monetary equivalent(s)].

Section 35 (e):

Zakāt is obligatory on gold and silver [and their monetary equivalent(s)] once two conditions are fulfilled;

1. That a lunar year elapses and the owner is in full possession of the gold, silver, [and/or their monetary equivalent(s)], &;
2. That the gold, silver, [and/or their monetary equivalent(s)] constitute the minimum zakāt payable amount or above.

Section 35 (f):

The minimum zakāt payable amount, for gold is 84.7 grams; for silver it is 592.9 grams; thus for money, one would find out the value of either gold or silver of their particular currency, and this would be the minimum zakāt payable amount. Once this is established the amount one must pay is 2.5 percent (if the *niṣāb* is arrived at, otherwise no payment is due).

Section 35 (g):

There is no zakāt on jewellery *(ḥulī al-mubāḥ)* that is in use, unless the owner intends to store it and not wear it.

Food Crops *(mu'ash-sharāt)*

Section 35 (h):

This constitutes fruits, which are raw dates and grapes once dried i.e. raisins and dry dates, and grain that is considered consumable and storable, such as rice, wheat, lentils etc.

SECTION 35 (I):

The minimum zakāt payable amount is 609.84 kilograms (*khamsa ausuq*). The amount one pays on crops, that have been naturally irrigated with no effort from the owner, such as rainwater, is 10 percent; whereas if effort was incurred, such as the use of machinery, or a water wheel then 5 percent is due.

Trade Merchandise *('urūḍ al-tijāra)*

SECTION 35 (J):

Zakāt on trade merchandise is subject to seven conditions:

1. That it is deemed merchandise;
2. That one intends to trade;
3. That the intention coincides with one's acquisition of the goods;
4. That one acquired the goods via transaction;[61]
5. That the trade merchandise does not become hard cash;
6. That the owner does not intend storage of the merchandise during the course of the lunar year, &;
7. That a lunar year elapses from the time of acquisition;

61 As opposed to inheriting the merchandise, or being given the merchandise as a gift or the like.

Section 35 (k):

The minimum zakāt payable amount, and the amount paid, correspond to that of gold and silver (as previously mentioned).

Buried Gold & Silver *(rikāz)*

Section 35 (l):

Zakāt is incumbent once four conditions are fulfilled:

1. That it be gold, or silver (thus jewels and the like are exempt);
2. That is reaches the minimum zakāt payable amount;
3. That it was buried in pre-Islamic times, &;
4. That it is found on unowned land, or land owned by the one who found the gold or silver.

Section 35 (m):

The zakāt that one pays is 20 percent, and the minimum zakāt payable amount corresponds to that of gold or silver [as mentioned above].

Mined Gold & Silver *(m'adin)*

Section 35 (n):

Zakāt is incumbent once two conditions are fulfilled:

1. That it reaches the minimum zakāt payable amount;
2. That it is gold or silver (thus jewels and the like are exempt).

Section 35 (o)

The minimum zakāt payable amount, and amount paid corresponds to gold or silver [as mentioned above].

Section 36: **Zakāt al-Fiṭr**

Section 36 (a):

Zakāt al-Fiṭr corresponds to 2.03 litres from the staple food stock of a specific locale.

Section 36 (b):

It is incumbent once three conditions are fulfilled:

1. That one is Muslim;
2. That one grasps part of the last day of Ramaḍān, and part of the first day of Shawwāl (even if it be a moment of each day);
3. That the amount due is in excess of one's needs, and the needs of whom one provides for on the day of Eid, also in excess of one's debts and housing expenditure.

Section 37 (c):

Zakāt is only accepted if paid to the eight categories of people stated in the Qur'ān [9:60]. The categories are:

1. The poor (*fuqarā*);
2. The needy (*masākīn*);[62]
3. Zakāt workers (*'āmilūn*);
4. Those requiring reconciliation (*muallafa al-qulūb*);
5. One purchasing one's own freedom (*fī al-riqāb*);
6. Debtors (*gārimīn*);
7. Those fighting jihād voluntarily (*fī sabīl Allah*), &;
8. Travellers in need of money (*ibn al-sabīl*).

[62] The difference between someone 'poor' (*faqīr*) and one 'needy' (*miskīn*) is that a poor person, for example, is one who requires £1000 to cover his basic needs, but acquires less than half of this, whereas the latter requires £1000 to meet his basic needs, and finds more than half, but less than the total amount required.

THE BOOK OF FASTING

TAKEN FROM THE TEXT KĀSHIFAT AL-SAJĀ,
BY MUḤAMMAD NAWAWĪ AL-JĀWĪ.

SECTION 38: **Obligation to Fast**

فصل : يجب صوم رمضان بأحد أمور خمسة : أحدها بكمال شعبان ثلاثين يوماً وثانيها برؤية الهلال في حق من رآه وإن كان فاسقا وثالثها بثبوته في حق من لم يره بعدل شهادة ورابعها بإخبار عدل الرواية موثوق به سواءً وقع في القلب صدقه أم لا أو غير موثوق به إن وقع في القلب صدقه وخامسها بظن دخول رمضان بالاجتهاد فيمن اشتبه عليه ذلك

SECTION 38/38A

SECTION 38 (A):

Fasting the month of Ramaḍān becomes obligatory by one of five instances:

1. On completion of the month of Sha'bān thirty days;
2. Sighting the new crescent moon (*al-hilāl*), for the one who sighted it even if he were deviant (*fāsiq*);

3. Sighting the new crescent moon by an upright witness [63](*'adl al-shahāda*) making fasting incumbent on those who did not observe it;[64]
4. Being informed by an upright transmitter (*'adl al-riwāya)* who is reliable, whether one believes him or not,[65]or if one believes him however he is (deemed) unreliable, [66]or;
5. If one assumes that Ramaḍān has entered by way of ijtihad, if one is compelled to perform ijtihād.[67]

SECTION 39: **Conditions of Validity**

فصل شروط صحته أربعة أشياء: إسلام وعقل ونقاء من نحو حيض وعلم بكون الوقت قابلاً للصوم

---

[63] An 'upright witness' (*'adl al-shahāda*) is one who 'does not commit a major sin, nor persist upon a minor sin. Whose obedience outdoes his disobedience, and who is male, a free man, upright, a person of dignity, aware and has one's senses intact'.

[64] i.e. that he informed others of his sighting, thus making fasting obligatory upon those informed. The definition of an 'upright transmitter' (*'adl al-riwāya*) corresponds to that of an 'upright witness', excluding the traits of freedom and gender, thus the transmission of a slave or woman suffices.

[65] As he is known to be reliable, thus one must fast if informed by such a person.

[66] Based on the fact that one believes such a person.

[67] Such as one being imprisoned, or in a place where one has no track of time.

Section 39 (a):

There are four conditions for the validity of fasting:

1. Islam;
2. Sanity (*'aql*);
3. To be free from menstruation [and postnatal bleeding], &;
4. Knowledge that the days one fasts are valid fast-days;[68]

Section 40: **Conditions of Obligation**

فصل : شروط وجوبه خمسة أشياء : إسلام وتكليف وإطاقة , وصحة وإقامة Section 40/40a

---

Section 40 (a):

There are five conditions for who fasting is an obligation:

1. Islam;
2. Puberty and sanity (*taklīf*);
3. To be physically able[69] (*iṭāqa*);
4. Health;[70]&
5. Residency.[71]

---

[68] Thus to fast on days where fasting is invalid is impermissible, such as the days of Eid, or the eleventh, twelfth and thirteenth of Dhī al-Ḥijja *(Ayām al-Tashrīq)*.

[69] Thus fasting is not obligatory for one who is old and incapable, or a menstruating woman or the like.

[70] Thus fasting is not obligatory for one who is suffering from an ailment.

[71] Thus fasting is not obligatory for one travelling more than 81 kilometres (approx.).

SECTION 41: **Pillars of Fasting**

فصل: أركانه ثلاثة أشياء : نية ليلا لكل يوم في الفرض وترك مفطر ذاكرا
مختاراً غير جاهل معذور و صائم

SECTION 41 (A):

Fasting has three pillars:

1. To make the intention the night[72] prior to the fast-day, [and to do so] everyday for an obligatory fast;
2. Abstaining from that which invalidates the fast, whilst cognisant (*dhākir*), voluntarily (*mukhtār*), though not if one is excused out of ignorance (*jāhil m'adhur*),[73] &;
3. The one fasting.

SECTION 42: **Major Expiation** *(kaffāra al-'uẓma)*

فصل : ويجب مع القضاء للصوم الكفارة العظمى والتعزير على من أفسد
صومه في رمضان يوماً كاملا بجماع تام آثم به للصوم

---

[72] The intention is to be made after sunset (*maghrib*) and before true dawn *(fajr al-ṣādiq)* for the following day's fast.

[73] A person being excused out of not knowing a specific ruling *(jāhil m'adhur)* is defined in the books of jurisprudence as one who has recently accepted Islam or lives in a locale where he has no recourse to scholars.

Section 42 (a):

Major expiation, alongside making up a missed fast (*qaḍā*) and disciplinary action (*ta'zīr*)[74] are obligatory upon one who:

1. Broke one's fast;[75]
2. In the month of Ramadan;[76]
3. For a whole fast-day;[77]
4. By way of complete[78] sexual intercourse;[79]
5. Being intentionally sinful in one's fast.[80]

Section 43: **Making up Missed Fasts and Refraining from that Which Invalidates the Fast**

ويجب مع القضاء الإمساك للصوم في ستة مواضع : الأول في رمضان
لا في غيره على متعد بفطره و الثاني على تارك النية ليلا في الفرض Section 43/43A
والثالث على من تسحر ظانا بقاء الليل فبان خلافه الرابع على من أفطر

---

[74] *Ta'zīr* is disciplinary action for an infraction that otherwise has no defined legal punishment (*ḥadd*) nor expiation.

[75] Thus this excludes breaking another's fast, such as a traveller taking the dispensation (*rukhsa*) and then having intercourse with a fasting woman.

[76] Thus this excludes breaking one's fast, outside of the month of Ramaḍān, which does not result in major expiation.

[77] Thus this excludes one who, for instance, after breaking one's fast via sexual intercourse, became insane or died before sunset.

[78] i.e. entering of the glans, thus any less than this does not constitute sexual intercourse.

[79] Thus this excludes breaking one's fast through eating and the like.

[80] Thus this excludes one who committed sexual intercourse forgetfully, or assumed there was still time before the dawn entered etc.

ظانا الغروب فبان خلافه أيضا الخامس على من بان له يوم ثلاثين من
TION 43A شعبان أنه من رمضان والسادس على من سبقه ماء المبالغة من مضمضة
و إستنشاق

Section 43 (a):

Making up a missed fast, and refraining from that which breaks the fast (*imsāk*) in Ramaḍān, is obligatory in six instances, for:

1. One who intentionally breaks one's fast;
2. One who omits the intention the previous night for an obligatory fast;
3. One who eats assuming it is night time, but the opposite holds true;
4. One who eats assuming the sun has set, but the opposite holds true;
5. One who believes it to be the thirtieth of Sha'bān, but actually is the first of Ramaḍān, &;
6. One who was excessive in rinsing one's mouth, or one's nose, and water enters.

Section 44: **Invalidation of the Fast**

TION 4A فصل : يبطل الصوم بردة وحيض ونفاس أو ولادة وجنون ولو لحظة و
بإغماء وسكر تعدى به إن عما جميع النهار

Section 44 (a):

Fasting is invalidated by:

1. Apostasy;
2. Menstruation;
3. Post natal bleeding;
4. Birth;
5. Insanity, even momentarily;
6. Unconsciousness &;
7. Intoxication, if intentional, and if it lasted the whole day.[81]

فصل : الإفطار في رمضان أربعة أنواع : واجب كما في الحائض والنفساء
وجائز كما في المسافر والمريض ولا ولا كما في المجنون ومحرم كمن أخر قضاء
رمضان مع تمكنه حتى ضاق الوقت عنه

Section 44 (b): **Rulings of Breaking the Fast**

To break one's fast (*ifṭār*), in Ramaḍān, has four rulings:

1. Obligatory; such as for a female menstruating or bleeding postnatally;
2. Permissible; such as for a traveller or ill person;
3. Neither [obligatory nor permissible]; such as for an insane person;

---

[81] The author omitted other invalidators such as eating, drinking, intercourse, a substance that reaches one's orifice through an open passage, intentional vomiting and the like.

4. Impermissible; such as for one who delayed making up a previous obligatory fast, even though able to, until the time did not permit it.

وأقسام الإفطار أربعة أيضا : ما يلزم فيه القضاء والفدية وهو إثنان الأول
الإفطار لخوف على غيره والثاني الإفطار مع تأخير قضاء مع إمكانه حتى يأتي
'ION 44C رمضان آخر وثانيها ما يلزم فيه القضاء دون الفدية وهو يكثر كمغمىً عليه
وثالثها مايلزم فيه الفدية دون القضاء وهو شيخ كبير ورابعها لا ولا وهو
المجنون الذي لم يتعد بجنونه

SECTION 44 (C):

There are four categories in breaking one's fast (*ifṭār*):

1. Where making up a missed obligatory fast and expiation (*fidya*) are incumbent, this being two;

   (i) Breaking the fast out of fear for another,[82]&;
   (ii) Breaking the fast whilst delaying making it up, although able to, until the following Ramaḍān arrives.

2. Where making up a missed obligatory fast is incumbent, but not expiation. These are numerous, [as previously mentioned in Section 44 (A)] such as unconsciousness;

[82] Such as a breastfeeding woman, or pregnant woman, believing that fasting would be detrimental for the child or foetus.

3. Where expiation is incumbent, but not making up a missed obligatory fast. This is for an elderly person who is unable to fast, &;
4. Neither expiation, nor making up a missed obligatory fast. This is for one who is insane that does not instigate his insanity.

فصل : الذي لا يفطر مما يصل إلى الجوف سبعة أفراد ما يصل إلى الجوف بنسيان أو جهل أو إكراه وبجريان ريق بين أسنانه وقد عجز عن مجه لعذره وما وصل إلى الجوف وكان غبار طريق وما وصل إليه وكان غربلة دقيق و ذباباً طائراً أو نحوه. والله أعلم بالصواب

SECTION 44 (D):

There are seven instances where something that enters the orifice does not break the fast:

1. If something entered one's orifice forgetfully;
2. Or out of ignorance;
3. Or out of compulsion;
4. Saliva dislodging that which is between one's teeth, if one is unable to expel it, due to a valid excuse;
5. Dirt from the road entering one's orifice;
6. Remnants from sieving flour [or the like] entering one's orifice;
7. A fly or the like, whilst flying.

And God knows best what is correct.

نسأل الله الكريم بجاه نبيه الوسيم أن يخرجني من الدنيا مسلماً ووالديّ وأحبائي ومن إلى انتمى و أن يغفر لي ولهم مقحمات ولماً وصلى الله على سيدنا محمد بن عبد الله بن عبد المطلب بن هاشم بن عبد مناف رسول الله إلى كافة الخلق رسول الملاحم حبيب الله الفاتح الخاتم وآله وصحبه أجمعين والحمد لله رب العالمين

We ask God, the Generous, by the rank of His beautiful Prophet ﷺ to allow my parents, beloved ones, and descendants to leave this world as Muslims. To forgive their and my sins and indiscretions. And may the blessings of God be upon our Master, Muḥammad b. ʿAbdullah b. ʿAbd al-Muṭṭalib b. Hāshim b. ʿAbd Manāf, the Messenger of God to all creation, the Prophet of warfare, the beloved of God, the Opener, the Seal, and upon all of his Family and Companions. And all praise is for God, Lord of the Worlds.

NOTES

NOTES